For my brother David Gordon,
who suggested that I write this story.
Your idea and encouragement made this book possible.
Thank you.

Contents

A Confession

I recognize the fact that in real life goldfish cannot survive in the ocean's saltwater—and that fish really can't talk, either. ☺ This is an imaginary story meant to convey an important message. After all, Mickey Mouse, Shrek, Nemo, and Superman are invented characters as well.

Also, if you read this book to your children, please remind them not to take goldfish to the beach.

Introduction

If you are concerned about the future and anxious about your situation, I know how you feel. I lost my job in 2001 during the dot-com bust. The company was losing money faster than we could raise it and eventually the company sank faster than the Titanic. I thought it was the worst event of my life. I was two months away from being bankrupt. I had a wife, two young children, a mortgage, no health insurance, and very little savings. I was a paycheck away from losing it all. It *sounds* bad. It *felt* bad. Seen from one point of view I suppose it *was* bad. But one day I decided that I wasn't going to let this challenge take me down. And that's when I knew I had to change what I was thinking and doing.

I read a few books, which empowered me to take control of my financial future and helped me make some important decisions through the change. Eventually these decisions would lead to the work I do now as a writer, consultant, and speaker. I often joke that I went from Fired to Fired Up. My layoff led to my life's mission and purpose. What I thought was the worst event in my life actually lead to the best. I realized that dealing with waves of change is all about how we perceive and respond to the change we are facing.

Fast forward to today. I now do a lot of work with leaders and organizations to create positive change. With so many people and organizations affected by the current economy it occurred to me that we need a new model for dealing with the new waves of change in our work and in our lives. After all, *in today's world the cheese hasn't just been moved—it's been swept away by a tsunami of an economic crisis*. As a result, I felt compelled to write this book.

While on a plane traveling to speak to a commercial real estate company in California, I wrote this story. Four hours of divine inspiration later, *The Shark and the Goldfish* was born. It was an amazing experience. During my talk, I read a short version of the story and it was so well received that since then I have read it to thousands of people and the impact has been very exciting and encouraging. People are making real changes and experiencing real and positive results.

I know the story is simple. There are critics who mock simple books—they believe that books have to be long and complicated to be significant. But I have found that the closer we get to truth, the simpler and more powerful the lessons become. I think you will agree, and most of all I hope this book empowers you to take positive action to ride the waves of change in your life and at work.

There's a belief that most people embark on a quest to find their destiny. But more often than not, through adversity and challenges, our destiny finds us. It is during these times that we ask the important questions and make decisions that positively change the course of our lives. And I believe one of the most important questions you can ask is whether you are a shark or a goldfish. Which one are you?

Are You a Shark or a Goldfish?

Which one are you? Are you a Shark or a Goldfish? After reading this story, let us know at SG@jongordon.com.

We'd love to hear from you.

THE SHARK AND THE GOLDFISH

A Wave of Change

Gordy the goldfish lived a wonderful and simple life. He ate, slept, swam, and did twirls in the water any time his humans approached to feed him. He never wanted for anything, especially food. Food was abundant and he was prosperous. Life was good.

Then one day he was swept up in a net, put in a bag full of water, and carried to the beach by his boy. The boy wanted to play with his goldfish at the beach. So he dug a big hole in the sand, filled it with buckets of water, and placed his goldfish in his own private man-made lake. Laughter filled the air and everyone was happy.

That is, until a big wave came crashing onshore, flooding the boy's lake and taking the goldfish back into the ocean with it. The boy and his family ran into the water looking for their goldfish, but he was nowhere to be found.

Gordy cried for help but no one could hear him. And as he swam aimlessly in the ocean, tired, alone, and hungry, he wondered, "Who's going to feed me now?"

He was no longer safe and secure, and without food he would surely die. He decided to ask the other fish in the ocean if they would feed him, but they all laughed at him. "Silly goldfish," they said, "always waiting for someone to feed him."

6

The Shark and the Goldfish

Then just as Gordy was near collapse from the salt water and starvation, he met Sammy the Shark, who could only shake his head at the poor fellow. He was a *nice* shark and he hated seeing such a pathetic sight. He knew someone had to teach this fish how to fish. Plus, he felt that sharks got a bad rap and needed some positive publicity. It wasn't fair, after all, that humans thought all sharks were mean just because a few "Jaws" wannabes experience ocean rage and go off the deep end. All the sharks he knew were nice like him and just wanted to swim, eat food found in the ocean, and keep to themselves.

8

The Shark and the Goldfish

"Well, lookee here, my little friend. You know what your problem is?"

"Yes, I do," answered Gordy. "I'm starving and no one will feed me."

"No, that's not your problem," countered Sammy. "Your problem is that you are a goldfish. You are waiting to be fed. That's fine during the fat times when all sorts of people are feeding you. But you're in the ocean now. The free food has dried up. Times are a changin'. Things are a little tougher here. You have to work a little harder. You need to be a little smarter. You need to change your thinking. You need to become a shark. Goldfish wait to be fed. Sharks go out and find food. Now let me show you how to be a shark and we'll go to find food together."

And off they swam through the ocean of adversity and challenges and lean times to learn the art of finding food.

10

The Shark and the Goldfish

Embrace and Ride the Wave of Change

"So, is it easy being a Shark?" Gordy asked.

"It is if you know how to think and act," answered Sammy as they swam around a big coral reef. "Every day you have to choose whether you are going to be a shark or a goldfish—whether you are going to wait to be fed or whether you are going to find food. Each day you make this choice with your beliefs, thoughts, and actions. The choice is yours. What do you want to be? A shark or a goldfish?"

"Well, since I'm starving and won't make it here in the ocean as a goldfish, I'd better become a shark!

"Good," said Sammy. "I'm glad you said that. It's such an important principle that I'm going to write it in this coral reef here with one of my shark's teeth. That way if you forget the lessons I teach you or if you just need a reminder, you can always come back to this place. People always wonder why there are so many sharks' teeth on the beach. Well, now they know. It's because we love writing messages on rocks in the ocean. It's a good thing our teeth grow back or else we wouldn't be able to write or eat." Sammy wrote on the coral reef: "Shark or Goldfish: It's Your Choice" and it looked like this:

"Okay, I'm a shark now," said Gordy. "Now what do I do?"

"Now you find food," said Sammy. "That's what we do. We swim and we look for food. Preferably seafood. It's the healthy way to live and good for the heart."

"But how?" said Gordy, whose decision to be a shark was quickly replaced by fear and doubt. "I never had to find food before. I've always been fed."

"Let's face it, I'm not shark. I'm a goldfish and I might as well just give up now. I'm a realist and accept my fate. I believe the wave that brought me into the ocean was the end for me."

"Not so fast," Sammy said. "Goldfish may give up, but sharks don't. Don't throw in the towel just yet. Sure, a big wave brought you into the ocean, but it doesn't have to be to your demise. In fact, it could be a gift if you listen to old Sammy here. Sure, bad things happen. The world is not always a pleasant place. At times it seems like you are at the whim of the waves of change in your life. Waves hit.

They knock you down and throw you off balance. But I have a little secret that you need to know. It's a secret that highly successful sharks are fully aware of. It's so important I'm going to write it down for you."

"Are you joking?" Gordy asked. "After all, I'm a goldfish in an ocean with a shark who could make me his afternoon snack anytime he wants. What can I possibly control?"

"Oh, great question, my little appetizer—I mean, friend," Sammy said jokingly. "As a goldfish, you are right; there is little within your control. You swim around in your little safe world waiting to be fed. You read your humans' newspaper through the fishbowl while they read it. You listen to the music they listen to and twirl around when they come to say hello to you. There's not much you control. But remember—you are no longer a goldfish and you're not in your fishbowl anymore. You're in the ocean and you are on your way to becoming a nice shark like me. And this means you don't see yourself as a victim of circumstance. You don't believe that you are at the whim of the ocean and negative events. Rather, as a shark in training you believe you can influence your situation and your outcome by your positive thoughts, beliefs, and actions. Yes, it's true that you can't control the events in your life. You can't control the fact that you were hit hard by a wave of change. You can't control the fact that the free food has dried up. You can't control the actions of others. But you can control your positive thoughts and your positive responses to these events and challenges, and in turn this will determine the outcome. This principle is summed up by the Positive Shark Formula: Events (E) + Positive Response (P) = Outcome (O)."

"Does everyone know this formula?" Gordy asked.

"Unfortunately, they don't," answered Sammy. Too many fish allow the waves of life to crush them. Instead they must learn to ride them. The fact is, bad events happen to everyone. Everyone is tested in the ocean. Life is going to deal everyone waves of adversity and change, but what matters most is how you respond. For example, did you know there was a study conducted of the most successful and fulfilled sharks in the ocean? The researchers were surprised to learn that these highly successful sharks all had bad things happen to them, just like all the other fish in the ocean. But the successful ones did something different."

"What's that?" Gordy asked very curiously.

"They all used the *bad* event and turned it into *good.* While they were in the midst of their challenge they looked for the opportunity. As a result, they turned their misfortune into fortune. It's proof that the positive shark formula works."

"It's all about perspective, isn't it?" asked Gordy, who was starting to understand the power of the shark's teaching.

"Yes, it is," answered Sammy, who was glad Gordy hadn't given up yet.

"Everyone will experience waves of change throughout life. Some waves will be small and others will be so powerful they turn your world upside down. But regardless of the size of the wave, the key is how you face it. You can make a wave of change your enemy by resisting it, which is like trying to swim against it. Or you can embrace the change, make it your friend, learn from it, and ride the wave.

It was such an important principle that he wrote it down on the coral:

"But how do I embrace and ride a wave of change?" Gordy asked.

"You trust that adversity is not the end, but the beginning of something better and greater," Sammy answered. "You tell yourself a positive story. Instead of defining your life as a horror story you define it as an inspirational tale. And instead of seeing yourself as a victim you assume the role of a fighter and an overcomer. You believe everything happens for a reason and in the midst of your challenge, like the one you are facing now, you ask the right questions. You ask:

- What can I learn from this experience?
- How can I grow wiser, stronger and better because of it?
- What opportunities does it present?
- What do I want?
- What positive actions do I need to take?"

"But what if I don't know the answer to these questions right now?" asked Gordy.

"No problem," said Sammy. "Knowing the answers is not important right now. The key is to keep these questions in the back of your mind and seek the answers. Trust that the answers will be revealed to you as you embrace change as something that will lead to good in the future. You know, there is a myth," Sammy continued, "that most of us embark on a quest to find our destiny. But rather it is through challenges and change that our destiny finds us. It is during these times that we slow down, press the pause button of life, and ask the important questions I just shared with you."

"**It's almost as if the wave of change gives us the opportunity to start over,**" Gordy said.

"Yes, indeed," Sammy replied. "It's as if the wave of change washed everything away and now you get a fresh start and the opportunity to decide what you really, really want. You ask the most important questions and this leads to life-changing answers, actions, and positive change."

"I get it. I get it!" shouted Gordy, who was so excited he swam circles around the shark. "It's all starting to make sense. I'm not going to give up. I'm not going to be a victim. I'm ready to go find some food. I'm ready to start fresh."

"I'm excited that you're excited," Sammy said. "You are indeed ready to go find some food. Unfortunately, I can't go with you today. I have some errands to do. Got a family to take care of, you know. So why don't you take some time for yourself, utilize the principles we discussed, and we'll meet back here tomorrow. Okay?"

"Sounds great," said Gordy, who did a few twirls in the water, shouted, "I'll see you tomorrow," and raced off in search of food and a positive future. Along the way he picked up a shark's tooth, put it in his mouth, and wrote little notes on rocks to himself related to what he had just learned from Sammy. He wrote:

If you think your best days are
behind you, they are

If you think your best days are
ahead of you, they are

I accept the fresh start Ive been given

Ride the wave of change

Stay Positive

After writing notes on the rocks, Gordy swam in search of food. He found a morsel here and a morsel there, but nothing of substance. He remembered what Sammy had taught him. He was in control of his thoughts and actions, and so he kept swimming and hoping that he would find some food soon. But he couldn't help but consider that perhaps all the food in the ocean was gone for the day. Maybe all the other fish had taken their share and now there was nothing left for him. To make matters worse, the other fish laughed at Gordy as he swam past them. "Look at the goldfish trying to be a shark," they jeered. "Good luck finding some food. You're in way over your head. You'll never make it here. It's too hard. You don't have the skills needed to make it in the ocean. Go back to your fishbowl," they shouted.

Gordy felt defeated. Maybe they were right. Sure, he could choose to be a shark, embrace change, and take positive actions, but maybe he just wasn't cut out for the business of finding food. Maybe it was beyond him. Maybe dreams and destinies were meant for others, but not for fish like him. Maybe his destiny was to be in a fishbowl or wilt away in the ocean. He cried himself to sleep that night with an empty stomach and a mind full of doubt.

The next morning Gordy woke up early and went searching for food. He still had a glimmer of hope that he would find some and that Sammy would have some answers. Thankfully, there was more food in the ocean than there had been yesterday. It seemed getting up early made a difference. He found enough for him to survive, yet it still fell way short of what he needed to thrive. And so Gordy gave up the search for food and swam in search of Sammy and some answers. He found him at the same place where they had met the day before.

"I've been waiting for you," Sammy said.

"Why's that?" Gordy asked.

"Oh, just wanted to see how your search for food went yesterday."

"Not good at all," said Gordy, who then told Sammy what the other fish said to him and how it made him feel defeated. He shared with Sammy that perhaps he wasn't cut out for finding food. Sammy just sat there smiling.

"I had a feeling we would be having this conversation. It's part of the growth process. This is the part where knowing how to think and act must become what you really think and do. As I told you earlier, living in the ocean will test who you are and what you believe. Finding food is about more than embracing change and responding to negative events with a positive perspective. It is also about staying positive in the face of those I call the 'chorus of negativity.' They are the naysayers you interact with every day, the doubters who say you can't do it, writers of the *Ocean Gazette*, and the broadcasters of the Constantly Negative News channels.

"Unfortunately, little buddy, there are many in the ocean who want to focus on what they believe is impossible, not what is possible. They want to focus on the negative, not the positive. They are impossibility thinkers who believe that the ocean is a place where everything is scarce. They love to focus on stories that highlight how the ocean suffers from a lack of food, a lack opportunity, and a lack of hope. And then there are those like the ones you met yesterday, who tell you that you are not good enough, strong enough, or big enough to find food. They believe that success was meant for others, not for fish like you or them. They are imprisoned by their own limited thinking."

"So what do I do when their negativity makes me feel defeated?" Gordy asked. "There's so much negativity coming at me from all directions it seems impossible to overcome it."

"I know, little buddy. The ocean is a school and overcoming negativity is the ultimate test. And the answer to this test is the Power of Belief." Sammy wrote the following on the coral reef:

"All success starts with belief. After all, if you don't believe in yourself and you don't believe there's enough food in the ocean, you will never find it. You must believe in your ability to find food and you must also believe that there is plenty of food to be found. Then I am convinced you'll find all the food you want. You pass the test right here in your mind first. This leads to success in the ocean. Positive beliefs lead to powerful actions. When you choose to tap into the power of belief you'll realize a key lesson

I have found over the years." And Sammy wrote another message on the coral:

"That's why it's so important to stay positive," Sammy said. "You must stay positive in the absence of negativity and in the face of it."

"But what do I do when the chorus of negativity and doubt is directly in my face and so loud that I can't think?" Gordy asked.

"Well, then you have a simple choice. You can choose to listen to the cynics and doubters and believe that success is impossible or you can tune them out, strengthen your belief, and know that with faith and an optimistic attitude all things are possible. You can listen to all the negative voices or focus on your positive choices."

Gordy, who had never realized he had choices before, asked, "What choices?"

"I'm glad you asked," Sammy replied. "Now you are on your way to becoming a master of finding food. The first choice you have is a choice between faith and fear." He wrote on the coral:

"Do you know what fear and faith have in common?" asked Sammy.

"The letter F," answered Gordy.

"Nice try," said Sammy. "What fear and faith have in common is a future that hasn't happened yet. Fear believes in a negative future. Faith believes in a positive future. Interestingly enough, both believe in something that hasn't happened yet. So I ask you, if neither the positive or negative future has happened yet, why not choose to believe in a positive future? Why not believe that great things are coming your way? Why not have faith in the future and in your ability to create it? And yet, so many fish choose the negative future," continued Sammy. "They choose fear instead of faith. They choose to believe that their best days are behind them, not in front of them. They choose to believe in the chorus of negativity. As a result, this fear either paralyzes them from taking action to find food or causes them to swim frantically around the ocean wasting time and scattering their energy."

"But it's scary," countered Gordy. "There's fear of the unknown. Fear of change. Fear of failing. Fear of not being strong enough or fast enough or good enough. Fear of starving. Even fear of fear. There's a lot to be fearful of out there!"

"Of course it's scary," Sammy replied. "No one said living in the ocean was easy. That's why now more than ever, choosing faith is so important. Faith helps you overcome the fear that sabotages your joy and success. It helps you get through tough times when you just want to give up. Faith gives you energy and hope and inspiration. It allows you to be less stressed about life's challenges and better equipped for success. Your faith and belief in a positive future leads to powerful actions today. Because you believe in yourself and the future, you take the actions necessary to create it."

Gordy was so inspired that he grabbed a shark's tooth he found on the ocean floor, put it in his mouth, and wrote on the coral reef something he wanted to remember. He wrote:

"You can also choose how you see the ocean," Sammy said. "You can see it as a place of abundance or of scarcity. Whatever you believe, you will find. While others are paralyzed by fear and negative beliefs you go about your business of finding food. While others choose to focus on the stories that demonstrate a lack of food, opportunity, and hope, you stay positive, believe there is food to be found, continue searching for it, and then create your own positive story."

Then he wrote on the coral:

"You need to realize it's a big ocean out there. It's a vast place filled with energy, food, vitality, and life. Sure, you may have to move to a different part of the ocean. You may need to innovate and find a better way of finding food. But the key here is that the ocean is huge and full of resources and opportunity. Why choose to limit the possibilities when history has shown that anything is possible? Why shouldn't you be the one to find a new food location? Why shouldn't you be the one who discovers a new way of finding food? Why shouldn't you be the one who discovers a way to make more food available to more fish? You need to think big and expect there is enough for everyone, especially you. Expect success and you will find more of it."

Gordy understood everything Sammy was teaching him. But the fish who jeered at him yesterday had left him with a nagging negative feeling. If he could shake it he would, but the negativity lingered.

"What about those days when you don't find food," he asked, "and your mind fills up with negative thoughts, self-doubt, and the beliefs of others? How do I overcome the feeling of defeat I was hit with by the naysayers? What do I do when I just don't want to get up in the morning and face another day of failure?"

"Well, my little friend," Sammy said as he put his fin around Gordy, "You accept the fact that everyone gets down. Then you decide to pick yourself up and turn it around. To do that you do what you did this morning. You find the ray of hope and eternal optimism that exists inside you. It was planted in your heart to let you know you are more than your failures and greater than your defeats. When you don't feel like getting out there in the ocean, you tap into this ray of hope. It tells you that today will be better than yesterday and tomorrow will be better than today. You keep swimming forward with faith and optimism. Instead of starting your morning by turning on the negative news, consider taking a swim of prayer. Instead of listening to the chorus of negativity, take a swim, close your eyes, smell the seaweed, and discover the real peace and strength you seek. This is the antidote to fear and it is what you need in order to succeed right now."

Then Sammy lifted Gordy with his fin and propped him on his back and raced around the ocean at blistering speeds. Gordy laughed and cheered as he held on for an exhilarating ride. He was now more prepared and ready to find food.

Sammy had to take his kids to school and so Gordy was once again on his own in search of food. Along the way he wrote a few more notes to himself so he would have positive reminders the next time he faced the chorus of negativity.

The only one who can limit your possibilities is you

Don't let your past determine your future

Instead of being disappointed about where you are, be optimistic about where you are going

Gordy, loaded with positive energy and a new attitude, continued his search for food. As he swam around the ocean, he reminded himself that he was not a goldfish anymore. He was not a victim but an overcomer. He was faithful and fearless. He looked out into the ocean and realized how big it really was. Surely there is enough food for a little belly like mine, he told himself. This new approach and perspective energized him as he swam from place to place in search of food. Most importantly it helped him stay positive when he once again swam by the jeering fish who shouted insults at him. "Where are you going?" they yelled. "Back to your fishbowl! We thought we had seen the last of you." To make matters worse, they held up signs about the negative conditions in the ocean. The signs said:

Food supply down 10 percent.
Is this the end?

Chance of starving rises
from 6 percent to 10 percent.
What now?

Confidence index down 50 percent.
Are we headed for an ocean depression?

Gordy looked for a few seconds at the signs, but then chose to look away. He remembered what Sammy had said about tuning out the negative voices and focusing on the positive aspects. Even if the food supply is down 10 percent, it's still very high; and even though the chance of starving rose to 10 percent, there is still a 90 percent chance of not starving, he said to himself. In that moment he made a conscious decision to create his own positive story instead of listening to the negative comments of others. Instead of a feeling of defeat this time, he was empowered with a belief that there was food to be found and he would be the one who found it.

By the mid-afternoon his new attitude and perspective helped him find twice as much food as he had found yesterday. He decided he had enough to survive and made his way to a quiet place where he would relax and take the rest of the afternoon off. As he relaxed and reflected on his day, it occurred to him that while he was proud of his accomplishment—finding enough food to survive—and was thrilled that he was no longer starving, he still wasn't completely satisfied. He was still a little hungry and knew he could find even more food if he had the energy. He didn't just want to survive. If the ocean was a place of abundance, then he wanted to thrive. And as he dozed off to sleep, dreaming of finding piles and piles of food, he thought of a few questions he should ask Sammy the next day.

Thrive because of Change

After waking up early with the belief that he would find food, Gordy found enough for a light breakfast and made his way to Sammy's place, where Sammy was once again waiting for him.

"So, how'd it go yesterday?" Sammy asked.

"Really good," Gordy answered. "But—"

"But what?" Sammy asked.

"But I think I could find even more food. I've found enough to get by, but if I'm going to be a fearless shark then I want to do more than survive. I want to thrive. I don't know what I'm doing wrong."

"You're not doing anything wrong," Sammy said as he lifted Gordy with his fin, plopped him on his back, and started swimming faster and faster. "It's just that now you are at the point where your positive attitude must be enhanced by focus and action. A positive attitude will help you survive, but it's not enough. If you want to thrive, then you must not only think like a shark, but act like one, too."

"How's that?" Gordy asked.

"It's best to show you what I mean," Sammy said as he raced around the ocean with a focus and intensity unlike anything Gordy had ever seen. He found more food in an hour than Gordy caught all day. But he didn't stop there. He continued searching for food throughout the day, taking short breaks and then resuming his search with more focus and intensity than before. By the end of the day Sammy had found more food than Gordy had seen in a lifetime. He was amazed.

"You know what the difference between you and me is?" Sammy asked.

"Yeah, you're a lot faster and bigger than me," Gordy said.

"That's true," replied Sammy, "but that's not why I thrived today and you didn't yesterday. The difference lies in three simple but very important reasons.

"First, I bet I worked harder than you. Would you agree with that?"

"Yes, I would agree. I didn't know what hard work was all about until now," Gordy admitted. "I just swam around at a leisurely pace looking for food but now I see that if I want to thrive I need to step up my game."

"Indeed," Sammy said, as he nodded and wrote an important lesson for Gordy to remember.

"There's no denying it," Sammy said. "If you want to thrive you have to do more than just be positive. Being positive is essential and it's where all success starts. But to thrive you must work harder than everyone in the ocean. There's no substitute for hard work. Most fish want to think that I'm successful at finding food because I'm a shark. They think that I was chosen to find food and born lucky. But what they don't see is that I work harder than everyone. I believe the harder you work and the more positive you are, the luckier you become. I'm also more focused than they are and this is the second reason why I thrive. I focus more than others." He wrote on the coral once again:

"It's not just about working hard, but also focusing on what you want. Every day I ask myself, 'What do I want?' The answer, of course, is always food. So then I ask, 'What are the three most important things I need to do today that will help me find the food I desire?' Then, and most importantly, I tune out all the distractions that try to sabotage my success and I focus on taking action. I don't let all the irrelevant time and energy zappers get in the way of accomplishing my goal. I'm just more focused than the other fish," Sammy said.

"But weren't you born that way?" Gordy asked.

"Indeed I was," Sammy admitted. "Some are more focused than others, but focus is something that can be learned and applied. It is a skill. You just need to practice and commit to it. Everyone can learn to focus and when they do they'll start to thrive instead of merely survive."

Gordy nodded, knowing exactly what he needed to do. Instead of wandering around the ocean he needed to have a plan of action. He needed to identify what food he wanted to find, where he wanted to find it, and get better at finding it.

"So how do I get better at finding food?" he asked. "How do I find more food, more quickly?"

"Ah, great question fearless one. That is in fact the third reason why I thrive." He wrote on the coral:

Sammy continued, "I don't just work hard and focus on finding food; I work hard and focus on getting better at finding food. I have found that if you incrementally improve each day, each week, each month, and each year, you'll become one of the top food finders in the entire ocean. You can't settle for being average. You can't be satisfied with merely surviving. You have to work hard and focus on thriving."

"When did you stop searching for food yesterday?" Sammy asked.

Gordy hesitated, feeling ashamed. "Midafternoon," he said.

"That's okay," Sammy replied. "Now you know better. Now you know—you do not settle for anything less than a great day.

"You don't stop when you've found just enough to survive. You keep going until you thrive. You don't settle for being an average food finder. Each day you keep learning, growing, and improving. It may take you a while to become a great food finder like me, but *every day that you choose to work hard and not settle is a day that leads to the life that you want.* Most importantly, now is a time when those with a positive attitude, a desire to improve, a great work ethic, and an ability to focus will shine. The ocean is filled with food for those who are ready to work hard and find it. So, are you ready to go find some food?" Sammy asked.

"I'm ready," Gordy said.

And off they swam side by side with focus and intensity to find all the food that was available to them. Gordy wrote a few reminders along the way so as not to forget Sammy's important lessons. He wrote:

Know what you want, work hard,
and focus on getting it

Learn from others and model
their success

Over the next few weeks Gordy and Sammy spent every day together learning and practicing the art of finding food. Gordy experienced the power of Sammy's teachings as he found more and more food each day. He realized that you won't find food if you're not looking for it. While others were paralyzed by fear, he took action every day and his initiative helped him thrive. He also chose not to settle and made it a point to continuously improve and seek out new ideas and new strategies. He theorized that if you believed it was too late in life to create the life you want, then it was; but if you were willing to improve and learn a new skill, you would. Some of these new ideas came from Sammy and others came to him while he rested in the evening. He knew that no matter how much food he caught and how much he thrived he needed to stay humble and hungry. Humble enough to learn every day and hungry with a passion to become the best food finder he could be.

He was so thankful that Sammy had taught him everything he knew. Over the next few months, thanks to Sammy's teachings, Gordy became so skilled at finding food that he was eating more than he had when he was being fed by others. He realized that finding food made him stronger and wiser and more appreciative of the food he caught.

63

Thrive because of Change

He saw firsthand that the difference between a full and empty stomach were his positive beliefs and actions. And he also realized that there were far too many fish like him simply waiting to be fed. They were fearful, scared, and hungry just like he had been.

He wanted to give back and help others the way Sammy helped him. If he could change, he knew others could change, too. They just needed to be informed, empowered, and inspired the way he was. And so with Sammy's support and encouragement Gordy decided to start a shark school for goldfish. It was the least he could do.

A Shark School for Goldfish

Gordy opened his shark school and made it his mission to help other fish. He decided that if he truly believed the ocean was a place of abundance it was his duty to help others realize there was more food available for everyone. He also believed that the more you give the more you receive. It was a law of the ocean.

On the first official day of shark school, only 10 students showed up. Gordy taught them that the ocean is not your enemy, but your friend. He taught them that it is a place of abundance, not scarcity. He told them that in his school they would learn how to transform adversity into a wave of prosperity and he wrote a few important lessons on a big rock board:

The fish were amazed at his teachings and they went back to their families, friends, and communities and told everyone what they had learned. The following day hundreds of new students arrived at the shark school and Gordy taught them everything he knew. He taught the bottom feeders how to take initiative, he taught the naysayers to be more positive, he taught the octopus how to focus, and he taught everyone how to think and act like a shark. He wrote more lessons on the rock board:

After a year, Gordy had taught thousands of fish at his shark school. He knew, however, that his students represented only a small percentage of the total fish in the ocean. Gordy wished that even more fish would attend his school, but he knew that's the way it was. There would be those who would believe and receive his message and apply the principles and those who would ignore the teachings and spend a lifetime complaining, blaming, and wondering why they were starving.

But those who applied the principles and lessons would navigate the sea of adversity and waves of change and enjoy a full stomach and a life of abundance. He had seen it happen in his own life and knew that life was too short to live any other way.

The End.

Start Your Own Shark School for Goldfish

Empower Your Team to Ride the Waves of Change and Teach Them How to Fish

Now you can put the Shark and Goldfish Principles to work in your organization. Using proven principles and practical tools based on *The Shark and the Goldfish*, by Jon Gordon, you will inspire and empower your people to thrive during waves of change.

Our world-class facilitators are able to conduct workshops and training with everyone in your company at every level. From coaching leaders to enhancing the engagement of front-line employees, we focus on generating an immediate and positive impact as well as creating long-term sustainable change. As a result our clients don't just survive, they thrive during both bad and good times.

Visit www.SharkandGoldfish.com and empower your team.

- Send an e-rock with a positive message via e-mail.
- Print and share posters with lessons from the book.
- Use our free resources to help you launch a change initiative.
- Empower your team through a wave of change.
- Enhance morale, productivity, and performance.

Food for Thought

Individual/Small Group/Team Discussion Questions

Utilize the following questions to ride the waves of change in your life and work. While you can reflect on these questions by yourself it is recommended that you gather friends, coworkers, colleagues, and your team and discuss these questions together.

A Wave of Change

- Describe a time when you were hit with a wave of change. What kind of change was it? What happened?
- How did you feel? What did you think?
- How did you respond? Did it work?
- What kind of wave of change are you facing now?

- How are you dealing with it?
- In what ways are you being a shark or a goldfish?
- What are the benefits of being a shark versus a goldfish?

Embrace and Ride the Waves of Change

- What are the challenges associated with the change you are facing?
- Are you a hero or a victim? Why?
- Would you define your life as a horror movie or an inspirational story? Why?
- What can you learn from the challenges you are facing?
- How can you grow wiser, stronger, and better because of this wave of change?
- What opportunities does this wave of change present?
- What do you want? What is your vision?
- What is holding you back?
- What positive actions do you need to take?
- What will inspire you to take these actions?

- What is your *why?* What bigger purpose will inspire you to make a positive change?

Stay Positive

- In response to your wave of change, what types of negativity are you facing?
- Are you dealing with naysayers and doubters? What are they saying? How do they make you feel? How are you responding to them?
- Are you experiencing self-doubt? Do you believe in your ability to overcome the wave of change you are experiencing? Why or why not?
- Do you believe in an ocean of abundance or of scarcity? Why?
- What fears does this wave of change bring up for you? Are they holding you back? Why?
- What would be an effective way for you to face and overcome these fears? What is the antidote to the fear you are facing?
- How can optimism, faith, and hope overcome fear and create success?

Thrive because of Change

- What beliefs and actions will help you create the life that you want?
- Do you believe you have to work hard to be a success? Why or why not?
- What does hard work mean to you? Are you willing to work hard to thrive?
- In what ways do you need to improve your focus?
- What are three things you need to do each day to help you thrive?
- In what ways can you learn, improve, and grow?
- Who are several possible mentors you can connect with and learn from?
- Are you passionate and hungry about being the best you can be? Why or why not?
- What will it take to inspire you to be your best? What bigger purpose will inspire you?
- Are you ready to take action?

Other Books by Jon Gordon

The Energy Bus

A man whose life and career are in shambles learns from a unique bus driver and set of passengers how to overcome adversity. Enjoy an enlightening ride of positive energy that is improving the way leaders lead, employees work, and teams function.

www.TheEnergyBus.com

The No Complaining Rule

Follow a VP of Human Resources who must save herself and her company from ruin, and discover proven principles and an actionable plan to win the battle against individual and organizational negativity.

www.NoComplainingRule.com

Training Camp

This inspirational story about a small guy with a big heart, and a special coach who guides him on a quest for excellence, reveals the eleven winning habits that separate the best individuals and teams from the rest.

www.TrainingCamp11.com

Soup

The newly appointed CEO of a popular soup company is brought in to reinvigorate the brand and bring success back to a company that has fallen on hard times. Through her journey, discover the key ingredients to unite, engage, and inspire teams to create a culture of greatness.

www.Soup11.com

The Seed

Go on a quest for the meaning and passion behind work with Josh, an up-and-comer at his company who is disenchanted with his job. Through Josh's cross-country journey, you'll find surprising new sources of wisdom and inspiration in your own business and life.

www.Seed11.com

One Word

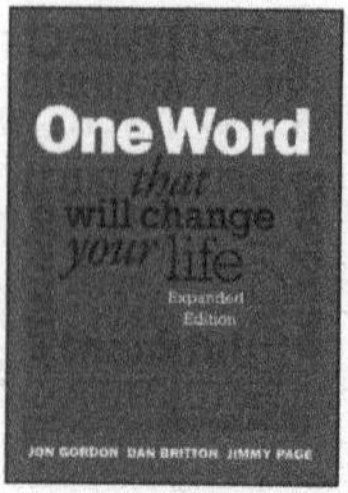

One Word is a simple concept that delivers powerful life change! This quick read will inspire you to simplify your life and work by focusing on just one word for this year. *One Word* creates clarity, power, passion, and life-change. When you find your word, live it, and share it, your life will become more rewarding and exciting than ever.

www.getoneword.com

The Positive Dog

We all have two dogs inside of us. One dog is positive, happy, optimistic, and hopeful. The other dog is negative, mad, pessimistic, and fearful. These two dogs often fight inside us, but guess who wins? The one you feed the most. *The Positive Dog* is an inspiring story that not only reveals the strategies and benefits of being positive, but also an essential truth: being positive doesn't just make you better; it makes everyone around you better.

www.feedthepositivedog.com

The Carpenter

The Carpenter is Jon Gordon's most inspiring book yet—filled with powerful lessons and success strategies. Michael wakes up in the hospital with a bandage on his head and fear in his heart after collapsing during a morning jog. When Michael finds out the man who saved his life is a carpenter, he visits him and quickly learns that he is more than just a carpenter; he is also a builder of lives, careers, people, and teams. In this journey, you will learn timeless principles to help you stand out, excel, and make an impact on people and the world.

www.carpenter11.com

The Hard Hat

A true story about Cornell lacrosse player George Boiardi, *The Hard Hat* is an unforgettable book about a selfless, loyal, joyful, hard-working, competitive, and compassionate leader and teammate, the impact he had on his team and program, and the lessons we can learn from him. This inspirational story will teach you how to build a great team and be the best teammate you can be.

www.hardhat21.com

You Win in the Locker Room First

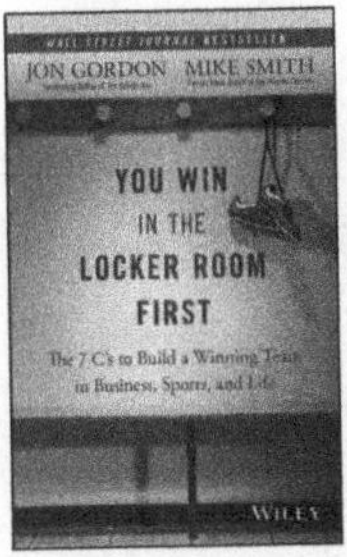

Based on the extraordinary experiences of NFL Coach Mike Smith and leadership expert Jon Gordon, *You Win in the Locker Room First* offers a rare, behind-the-scenes look at one of the most pressure-packed leadership jobs on the planet, and what leaders can learn from these experiences in order to build their own winning teams.

www.winthelockerroom.com

Life Word

Life Word reveals a simple, powerful tool to help you identify the word that will inspire you to live your best life while leaving your greatest legacy. In the process, you'll discover your *why*, which will help show you how to live with a renewed sense of power, purpose, and passion.

www.getoneword.com/lifeword

The Power of Positive Leadership

The Power of Positive Leadership is your personal coach for becoming the leader your people deserve. Jon Gordon gathers insights from his bestselling fables to bring you the definitive guide to positive leadership. Difficult times call for leaders who are up for the challenge. Results are the byproduct of your culture, teamwork, vision, talent, innovation, execution, and commitment. This book shows you how to bring it all together to become a powerfully positive leader.

www.powerofpositiveleadership.com

The Energy Bus Field Guide

The Energy Bus Field Guide is your roadmap to fueling your life, work, and team with positive energy. The international bestseller, *The Energy Bus*, has helped millions of people from around the world shift to a more positive outlook. This guide is a practical companion to help you *live and share* the ten principles from *The Energy Bus* every day, with real, actionable steps you can immediately put into practice in your life, work, team, and organization.

The Power of a Positive Team

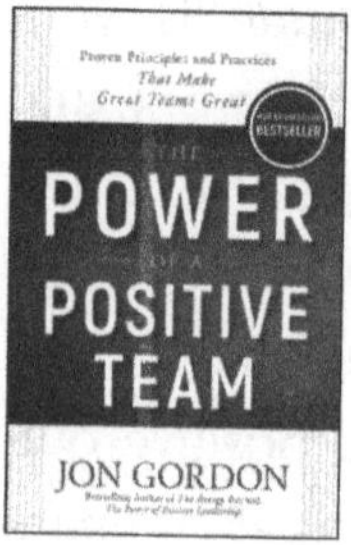

In *The Power of a Positive Team*, Jon Gordon draws upon his unique team building experience, as well as conversations with some of the greatest teams in history, to provide an essential framework of proven practices to empower teams to work together more effectively and achieve superior results.

www.PowerOfAPositiveTeam.com

The Coffee Bean

From bestselling author Jon Gordon and rising star Damon West comes *The Coffee Bean*: an illustrated fable that teaches readers how to transform their environment, overcome challenges, and create positive change.

The Energy Bus for Kids

The illustrated children's adaptation of the bestselling book, *The Energy Bus*, tells the story of George, who, with the help of his school bus driver, Joy, learns that if he believes in himself, he'll find the strength to overcome any challenge. His journey teaches kids how to overcome negativity, bullies, and everyday challenges to be their best.

www.EnergyBusKids.com

Thank You and Good Night

Thank You and Good Night is a beautifully illustrated book that shares the heart of gratitude. Jon Gordon takes a little boy and girl on a fun-filled journey from one perfect moonlit night to the next. During their adventurous days and nights, the children explore the people, places, and things they are thankful for.

The Hard Hat for Kids

The Hard Hat for Kids is an illustrated guide to teamwork. Adapted from the bestseller *The Hard Hat*, this uplifting story presents practical insights and life-changing lessons that are immediately applicable to everyday situations, giving kids—and adults—a new outlook on cooperation, friendship, and the selfless nature of true teamwork.

www.HardHatforKids.com

About the Illustrator

Artist-Animator-Musician

Donald Wallace has dedicated his entire life to art and music. He applies his artistic abilities in all areas of the media producing cartoons, illustration, animation, movie concept art, and graphic design. Whether designing and producing for computer animation, animating in the traditional hand-drawn style, creating digital illustration for the print and Internet markets, or developing cartoon characters and concept design, there isn't much he hasn't experienced in his career. Artistically, he has been involved in four music video productions, directed art and animation for several CD-ROM games, and designed, produced, and directed hundreds of commercials for television. Musically, he is currently composing instrumental works and developing a musical play. He lives and works in Portland, Oregon, with his wife Kelly, and their cat Toonces. He can be reached at 503-224-9660.